Thomas Jefferson and His Unknown Brother

A Map

Showing places mentioned in the letters,
after Thomas Jefferson's map of 1786
made for his Notes on Virginia.

Thomas
Jefferson
and His
Unknown
Brother

Edited and introduced by BERNARD MAYO
with additions by JAMES A. BEAR, JR.

UNIVERSITY PRESS OF VIRGINIA
Charlottesville

THE UNIVERSITY PRESS OF VIRGINIA
Copyright © 1981 by the Rector and Visitors
of the University of Virginia

This edition first published 1981

Library of Congress Cataloging in Publication Data
Jefferson, Thomas, Pres. U.S., 1743–1826.
  Thomas Jefferson and his unknown brother.

  The 32 letters reproduced here are the only extant
correspondence from the 50 or more letters written
between 1789 and 1815. Most are from the Carr-Cary
papers of the McGregor Library, University of Virginia,
3 are from the Massachusetts Historical Society, and
1 is from the Library of Congress.
  1. Jefferson, Thomas, Pres. U.S., 1743–1826.
2. Jefferson, Randolph, 1755–1815. 3. Virginia—
Social life and customs. 4. Presidents—United States
—Correspondence. I. Jefferson, Randolph, 1755–1815.
II. Mayo, Bernard, 1902–1980. III. Bear, James Adam, Jr.
IV. Virginia. University. Library. Tracy W. McGregor
Library. V. Title.
E332.88.J4 1981   973.4'6'0924 [B]   80–25272
ISBN 0–8139–0890–6

Printed in the United States of America

CONTENTS

Preface   vii

Jefferson's Unknown Brother   1

Genealogical Chart   8

Letters   13

PREFACE

The thirty-two letters reproduced here are the only extant correspondence from the fifty or more letters that passed between Thomas and his "unknown" brother Randolph between 1789 and 1815.

Most of the letters are printed with the permission of the Tracy W. McGregor Library, University of Virginia, from its Carr-Cary Papers; those of January 11, 1789, February 28, 1790, and February 9, 1807, are printed with permission from the Massachusetts Historical Society; and that of September 25, 1792, is from the Library of Congress.

Even with something less than half of their correspondence available, there is no difficulty in drawing a clear picture of Randolph and his relations with his older brother, Thomas. The latter is depicted as the enlightened resident of Monticello, while Randolph emerges at best as an unenlightened and simple dirt farmer, albeit one with an appreciable slave force and very valuable lands.

One is moved by Randolph's plaintive and ungrammatical pleas, reports, and requests to his brother for his watch (which both correspondents refer to as a "she"), a loan, or simply a letter. Thomas remains the superior, didactic, but sympathetic and very generous brother, who was equally adept in supplying Randolph with dogs, seed, advice on how to farm, or an admonition to use the bougie (which he supplied) even though it might be painful.

This brief correspondence contains little of real historical significance. It allows Randolph Jefferson an entrance to the American historical scene, a place that would have otherwise been denied him, had he so desired. It further illustrates that great contrasts, can, and do, exist between members of a family. And finally it illuminates Thomas Jefferson as a brother.

JAMES A. BEAR, JR.
Monticello

Thomas
Jefferson
and His
Unknown
Brother

JEFFERSON'S UNKNOWN BROTHER

Randolph Jefferson, born October 1, 1755, at Shadwell in Albemarle County, was twelve years younger than Thomas. With his twin sister, Anna Scott, or Nancy as she was known in the family, he was the last of ten children born to Jane Randolph and Peter Jefferson. He was two years old, and Thomas fourteen, when their father died suddenly August 17, 1757.

Peter Jefferson left a substantial estate and one unencumbered with debt. To each of his daughters he bequeathed £200 and a slave; his wife received a life estate in the Shadwell farm and slaves. The land, of course, went to the sons. By the terms of the will, Thomas, at his majority plus six months, was to have the choice of either the "Fluvanna lands" which lay generally in southern Albemarle County along the James River and its branches or the "Rivanna lands" centered at Shadwell in central Albemarle along the Rivanna River and its branches.

Thomas chose the latter, which amounted to about 2,650 acres in these tracts: a 1,000-acre farm that became Monticello; Shadwell, a 400-acre farm (which was to go to Thomas at his mother's death); Portobello, a farm of 150 acres which was later incorporated into the Tufton farm; another 150-acre division, also to become a part of Tufton; and a detached tract of 300 acres called Pouncey's. Randolph's patrimony, the "Fluvanna lands," amounting to 2,291⅔ acres of superior farmland, was composed of these elements: houses and 225 acres on the south side of the James River opposite the ferry landing at Scott's Ferry; 66⅔ acres on the north side of the Hardware River (these Jefferson purchased in 1796);

and the Snowden, or home tract, of 2,050 acres with a house in Buckingham County. There was also an equitable division of slaves, with each son receiving about twenty. Peter Jefferson's other land was sold by his executors.

While Thomas was being boarded and schooled by the Reverend James Maury, Randolph was being instructed by Benjamin Snead. Snead's school was located a few miles southeast of Shadwell at the Buck Island plantation of Charles Lewis, Jr., whose wife was Randolph's aunt. During these years the accounts of John Harvie, Peter Jefferson's principal executor, show payments to Charles Lewis for Master Randolph's board and tuition to Snead. Meanwhile, Thomas went on to the College of William and Mary, then studied law under George Wythe, and began the practice of law in 1767. In that year Harvie died. Thenceforth Thomas with a brotherly affection began to look after Randolph's interests.

At sixteen Randolph was sent to Williamsburg for further schooling. It is unclear from the few records (which include the bursar's books at the College of William and Mary) whether he attended the grammar school, the college, or both. According to Jefferson's records, Randolph left Shadwell for Williamsburg on October 1, 1771, arriving in time to begin his instruction with the Reverend Thomas Gwatkin, professor of natural philosophy and mathematics. After ten months with Professor Gwatkin, Randolph appears to have been entered in the grammar school, then headed by Josiah Johnson, with its less rigorous curriculum. College records only reveal that he was under schooling in 1771 and 1772; unfortunately they fail to say in which schools.

Randolph was back in Albemarle by October or November 1772, for on January 26, 1773, Thomas Jefferson paid William Page for transporting his bed and trunk from Williamsburg to Shadwell. Of Randolph's scholastic record nothing is known; his letters, however, furnish strong evidence that he was not a strong student.

Even less is known of Randolph's social life while in the Virginia capital, but the supposition is that it in no way resembled that enjoyed by his brother, who often dined with Dr. William Small, George Wythe, and Francis Fauquier and frequently attended Governor Fauquier's soirees, long noted for their Attic wit and chamber music. A May 3, 1774, entry in Jefferson's daily memorandum books reveals that Randolph took violin lessons from Francis Alberti, who had also instructed Thomas, suggesting that in some degree he shared his brother's passion for the sound of music.

These memorandum books and another of Thomas's records, the fee book and miscellaneous accounts, are excellent financial records of the relationship of the two men. Their entries concern Randolph's education, his lands, sale of his tobacco crops, and various other business transactions. They also reflect the deep and personal interest Thomas took in Randolph's affairs both before and after he came of age.

During the Revolution, Randolph served, presumably as a private soldier, in General Thomas Nelson's corps of Virginia Light Dragoons. It is supposed that he served under Charles Lewis of North Garden, who for a time was colonel of the Fourteenth Virginia Regiment. In 1778 he also saw active service as a member of a troop of Albemarle County light horse in the northwest. With

Colonel Lewis, Thomas Jefferson, and other determined patriots of Albemarle County, he signed the special Oath of Allegiance to the Commonwealth of Virginia (the so-called Albemarle Declaration of Independence), of April 21, 1779. During the British invasion of 1781, his plantation Snowden furnished provisions for Virginia troops, pasturage for cavalry horses, and Negro laborers who helped remove military stores from Scott's Ferry. When the victory at Yorktown that fall brought an end to military alarums and excursions, Randolph settled down at Snowden as a farmer whose life, in sharp contrast to that of his distinguished brother, was narrowly circumscribed physically as well as intellectually.

On July 30, 1780, he married Anna Jefferson Lewis, the daughter of Colonel Charles Lewis, Jr., of Buck Island. She was his first cousin, and the sister of Charles Lilburne Lewis, who in 1769 had married Randolph's sister Lucy. The Lewis and Randolph Jefferson families became even closer when Randolph's son Thomas Jefferson, Jr., married Mary Randolph Lewis, Lucy Jefferson Lewis's daughter. By his first wife, who died sometime before 1808, Randolph had five sons, Isham Randolph, Thomas, Jr., Field, Robert Lewis, and James Lilburne, and one daughter, Anna Scott. His second wife, Mitchie B. Pryor, was the daughter of David Pryor of Buckingham County. They were married, probably in 1809, and by her he had but one son, John. It was Randolph's children, rather than Thomas's, who carried on the Jefferson family name.

Although Thomas Jefferson's brother took no part in politics, he was commissioned a captain of Buckingham

County militia in 1794. Captain Jefferson, as he was commonly called, was a substantial farmer. His Buckingham County taxes for 1782 reveal an assessment based on thirty slaves, six horses, forty-two cattle, and 2,000 acres of land. In 1815, the year of his death, he possessed twenty-two slaves, six horses, twenty-five cattle, and 1,827 acres of land.

From boyhood Randolph was often in debt (as was his brother), and his second wife was an extravagant and difficult woman who ran up large bills with the merchants of Warren and Scott's Ferry. His last years were distressed by extreme friction between his wife and sons. The latter were highly incensed when their stepmother succeeded in having their father make a new will which was greatly in her favor and to their detriment. In the opinion of Joseph C. Cabell, the second Mrs. Randolph Jefferson was a "Jade of genuine bottom."

Randolph's health is as little known as his finances. These letters indicate that he was moderately healthy for the time, but that he experienced several serious illnesses, one of which was the "gravil," no doubt kidney stones. In another letter he reports that he has stopped imbibing alcoholic beverages. The cause of his death at Snowden on August 7, 1815, while in his sixtieth year remains yet another of Randolph's secrets. The lack of entries in Thomas Jefferson's memorandum books for the period August 8–10 is evidence that he probably accompanied Anna Scott Marks to Snowden for Randolph's final illness, death, and funeral. Randolph was probably buried at Snowden; however, no site is evident there today.

Before Randolph's death his sons and friends urged Jefferson to come to Snowden to assist in making Randolph change his will, but to no avail. In the contest that continued long after his death, his sons obtained a deposition from Jefferson which stated that their father throughout his life had always been in the habit of consulting his older brother "in all cases of importance respecting his interests. The one exception being his second marriage to Mitchie B. Pryor." The deposition went on to state that Randolph had never been skilled in managing his affairs and that "in all occasions of a life of diffidence in his own opinions, an extreme facility and kindness of temper, and an easy pliancy to the wishes and urgency of others, made him very susceptible of influence from those who had any views upon him."

BIBLIOGRAPHICAL NOTE

Peter Jefferson's family is listed in Jefferson's prayer book (original in the University of Virginia Library), printed as *Thomas Jefferson's Prayer Book* with an introduction by J[ohn] C[ook] W[yllie] (Charlottesville, Va., 1952). Information on Peter Jefferson's Fluvanna landholdings may be reviewed in the folder on Peter Jefferson in the Monticello Archives and in Edgar C. Hickisch's "Peter Jefferson, Gentleman," written for presentation as a requirement for a Ph.D. degree in history at the University of Virginia; his will is in Albemarle County Will Book II, pp. 32–35, Albemarle County Courthouse, Charlottesville, Va. A survey of Snowden made July 18, 1799, is in the Buckingham County Courthouse, Buckingham, Va. Unfortunately most of the Buckingham County records were destroyed in the fire of 1869. There are photostat copies at the University of Virginia Library of John Harvie's account books for 1757–65 (originals for 1757–65 in the Huntington Library, San Marino, Calif.); originals for 1759–61 at the Massachusetts Historical Society, Boston; of Thomas Jefferson's memorandum books for 1771, 1772, 1774, 1776–1778 (originals at the Massachusetts Historical Society), and 1773 (originals in the Library of Congress); and of Jefferson's fee book and miscellaneous accounts (originals in the Huntington Library), where are to be noted Randolph Jefferson's accounts and the account of the estate of Peter Jefferson.

Randolph Jefferson is listed without rank in John H. Gwathmey, *Historical Register of Virginians in the Revolution* (Richmond, 1938), p. 415, and as a signer of the "Oath of Allegiance Signed by Citizens of Albemarle County" [1771] in *The Papers of Thomas Jefferson*, ed. Julian P. Boyd and others (Princeton, N.J., 1950), 2: 128–30. This so-called Declaration of Independence was really an oath of allegiance to the new government. Randolph's claims for provisions, etc., furnished during the Revolution and his militia commission of May 13, 1794, as well as the Buckingham Land and Personal Property Tax Books for 1782 and 1815, are in the Virginia State Library in Richmond. Genealogical information, incomplete and sometimes conflicting, may be reviewed in Edgar Woods, *Albemarle County in Virginia* (1932; reprinted Bridgewater, Va., 1956), pp. 237–38; a genealogical chart of several generations of the descendants of Thomas Jefferson, Jr., is in *Report of Curator* to Trustees of the Thomas Jefferson Memorial Foundation (Charlottesville, Va., 1968), pp. 11–12, 24. Randolph's will (a draft) made May 27, 1808, is in the Carr-Cary Papers, Tracy W. McGregor Library, University of Virginia.

Perhaps the best source of biographical information on Randolph Jefferson is his folder in the Monticello Archives.

Peter Jefferson m. Jane Randolph

Jane	Mary m.	Thomas m.	Elizabeth	Martha m.
	John Bolling	Martha Wayles Skelton		Dabney Carr
	Martha m.	Martha m.		Jane Barbara m.
	Field Archer	Thomas Mann Randolph		Wilson M. Cary
	John m.	Jane Randolph		Lucy m.
	—— Kennon	Son		Richard Terrell
	Edward m.	Mary m.		Polly
	Dolly Payne	John Wayles Eppes		Peter m.
	Archibald m.	Lucy Elizabeth		Hetty Smith Stevenson
	Catherine Payne	Lucy Elizabeth		Samuel m.
	Mary m.			Eleanor B. Carr
	Edward Archer			Dabney m.
	Robert m.			Elizabeth O. Carr
	Jane Payne			
	Jane			
	Thomas			
	Ann			

Genealogical Chart

Peter Field	Son	Lucy m.	Anna Scott m.	Randolph m.

Lucy m.
Charles Lilburne Lewis
  Randolph m.
    Mary Howell Lewis
  Jane Jefferson m.
    Craven Peyton
  Isham m.
    ——— ?
  Charles
  Anna Marks
  Elizabeth
  Martha Ann Cary m.
    Daniel Monroe
  Lucy B. m.
    Washington Griffin
  Mary R. m.
    Thomas Jefferson, Jr.
  Lilburne m.
    1. Elizabeth Jane Woodson Lee
    2. Letitia Griffin Rutter

Anna Scott m.
Hastings Marks

Randolph m.
1. Anna Jefferson Lewis
  Isham Randolph
  Thomas Jefferson, Jr., m.
    1. Mary Randolph Lewis
    2. Elizabeth Siegfried Baker
    3. Nancy W. Pollard
  Field
  Robert Lewis m.
    M. Jordan
  James Lilburne
  Anna Scott m.
    Col. Zachariah Nevil
2. Mitchie B. Pryor
  John

LETTERS

Thomas Jefferson to Randolph Jefferson

Paris   January 11. 1789

Dear Brother

The occurrences of this part of the globe are of a na-
ture to interest you so little that I have never made them
the subject of a letter to you. Another discouragement
has been the distance and time a letter would be on it's
way. I have not the less continued to entertain for you
the same sincere affection, the same wishes for your
health and that of your family, and almost an envy of
your quiet and retirement. The very short period of my
life which I have passed unconnected with public business sufficed to convince me it is the happiest of all
situations, and that no society is so precious as that of
one's own family. I hope to have the pleasure of seeing
you for a while the next summer. I have asked of Congress a leave of absence for six months, and if I obtain it
in time, I expect to sail from hence in April, and to return in the fall. This will permit me to pass two months
at Monticello during which I hope I shall see you and
my sister there. You will there meet an old acquaint-
ance, very small when you knew her, but now of good
stature.[1] Polly you hardly remember and scarcely recol-
lects you.[2] Both will be happy to see you and my sister,[3]
and to be once more placed among their friends. They
will remain in Virginia, and are happy in the idea.
Nothing in this country can make amends for what one
loses by quitting their own. I suppose you are by this
time the father of a numerous family, and that my name-
sake is big enough to begin the thraldom of education.[4]
Remember me affectionately to my sister, joining my
daughters therein, who present their affectionate duty to

you also: and accept yourself assurances of the sincere attachment and esteem of Dear brother Your's affectionately,

Th:Jefferson

[1]Martha Jefferson, Thomas Jefferson's oldest daughter, was only twelve years of age when Randolph last saw her.

[2]Mary Jefferson, a younger sister of Martha, was born in 1778.

[3]Thomas Jefferson generally referred to in-laws such as his brother's wife as his sister. In this case the individual was Anna Jefferson Lewis (Mrs. Randolph) Jefferson.

[4]Thomas Jefferson, Jr., was Randolph Jefferson's second son.

Monticello   Feb. 28. 1790.

Dear brother

I will give the orders as you desire to George,[1] relative to peach stones and the puppies.[2] I send you by Orange[3] some very fine Apricot and Plumb stones to be planted immediately and to be cracked before they are planted. I have settled the administration of my sister Elizabeth's estate whereon you are to receive as follows.[4]

	Principal	Interest	
From J. Bolling[5] (order now inclosed)	£ 4–0–6	3–16– 8	interest from Jan.11. 1771
Colo. Chas. L. Lewis[6] (order inclosed)		8–11– 0	int. from Jan. 1. 1773.
Colo. N. Lewis[7] (order inclosed)	15–6–9	4–12– 3	
	19–7–3	16–19–11	

		£
or in a plainer form you will receive from	J. Bolling	7–17–2
	C. L. Lewis	8–11–0
	N. Lewis for me	19–19–0
	in the whole	36– 7–2

I have the pleasure further to inform you that Doctr. Walker has no right to call on us for any interest.[8] I have examined his account accurately with respect to that and find that charging him interest for the monies of the estate which he had at different times in his hands, and allowing him interest whenever the balance is in his favor, the result is that he would owe us a small balance of interest not worth notice: so there is an end of that matter. Give my love to my sister and the little ones. I am Dear brother yours affectionately,

Th:Jefferson

[1]This is probably the slave "Great" George who worked as a laborer in the ground and managed the Monticello nailery.

[2]Randolph obviously had asked for one of the pups of the shepherd dogs that Jefferson had purchased at Le Havre just before departing from France. They were of the Briard breed, and the bitch was Bergere.

[3]Orange was listed in the inventory of Peter Jefferson's estate as a boy worth £18. He was inherited by Randolph; he married Dinah, a slave of Thomas Jefferson, in 1761.

[4]For Thomas Jefferson's administration of his sister Elizabeth's estate, see Fee Book and Miscellaneous Accounts, 1767–74. This same source also has Randolph Jefferson's account.

[5]John Bolling had married Mary Jefferson on January 24, 1760.

[6]Charles Lilburne Lewis had married Lucy Jefferson on September 12, 1769.

[7]Colonel Nicholas Lewis, a friend and neighbor of Jefferson, resided at The Farm situated just below Monticello.

[8]Dr. Thomas Walker of Castle Hill was a neighbor and an executor of Peter Jefferson's estate and one of Thomas Jefferson's guardians.

Thomas Jefferson to Randolph Jefferson

Monticello   Sep. 25. 1792.

Dear Brother

Finding it necessary to sell a few more slaves to accomplish the debt of Mr. Wayles to Farrell & Jones,[1] I have a thought of disposing of Dinah and her family.[2] As her husband lives with you I should chuse to sell her in your neighborhood so as to unite her with him. If you can find any body therefore within a convenient distance of you who would be a good master, and who wishes to make such a purchase, I will let her and her children go on a valuation by honest men either there or here. One half the money to be paid within a year, the other within two years, and if not paid at the day interest to run from the date of the bond. Good security would be required. Dinah is 31 years old and two children are to go with her, to wit Sally 12. years old and Lucy whose age I do not know. Dinah is a fine house wench of the best disposition in the world and tho' she has worked out ever since I went to Europe, she would still suit any person for house business. If you can find a purchaser write me a line and send it to Mr. Randolph[3] and he will carry it to me immediately and an answer and proper orders shall be sent. I set out to Philadelphia the day after tomorrow to return finally in March. My love to my sister, and I am dear brother

Yours affectionately
Th:Jefferson

[1]John Wayles was the father of Martha Wayles Skelton Jefferson and Jefferson's father-in-law. Farrell & Jones was a British merchant firm to which Wayles's estate was heavily indebted. This debt was a part of Martha Jefferson's patrimony.

[2]Dinah was a Jefferson slave inherited from his father. Her husband was Orange. She was sold to James Kinsolving, who resided in the Mechum's River neighborhood in western Albemarle County.

[3]Thomas Mann Randolph was the husband of Jefferson's oldest daughter, Martha Jefferson Randolph. The Randolphs at this time lived at Edgehill, their farm which lay a few miles east of Monticello.

Thomas Jefferson to Randolph Jefferson

Washington   Feb. 9. 07.

Dear Brother

It was not until Mr. Randolph went home in December that I received your watch from Philadelphia.[1] The keeping her here has given me an opportunity of proving her and of being able to assure you that a better watch I believe was never made. I set her by a most accurate clock on New year's day, and she has varied but a minute and a half in that time, which is at the rate nearly of a minute a month. She cost something more than you limited. I paid 79½ Dollars for the watch, the chain, seal and key. You will have to make up the difference by some white clover seed. As I shall be at Monticello by the middle of March, I conclude to carry her myself so that you may recieve her there. This is the more necessary as it will be requisite to give you some information as to her management. In hopes I shall have the pleasure of seeing you then at Monticello. I conclude with my affectionate salutations and assurances of constant attachment.

Th:Jefferson

[1]The watch was purchased from Henry Voight, a well-known Philadelphia watchmaker.

Dear Brother

I should of wrote to you on this business before but wished to be certain in seeing whether I could procure the quantity of seed that I agreed with the nigroes for which was a bushel of Green soard and as much of White Clover they are now delivering that quantity at Eight shillings pr Gallon. I think the price high at that but I asure you that it was not in My power to git it cheaper if Convenient be pleased to inclose to Me as Much Money as will pay them of for there seed and send the letter on to warren[1] Where I Can receive it in any short time and you Will Very Much oblige your.—

Most affectionately.—
Rh; Jefferson
July 9th 07

P S
Be so good as to let Mr. Randolph know if he Wants to perchase either of those kinds of seed it Will be in My power to oblige him if he will write me immidiatily.—

[Addressed] Mr. Thomas Jefferson
pr son Lewis   monticello
To the Care of Mr. Dinsmore[2]

---

[1]Warren was a small settlement in southern Albemarle County situated at the confluence of Ballenger's Creek and the James River. A ferry crossed the river to Buckingham County at this point.

[2]James Dinsmore was one of the able carpenters who worked on the construction of Monticello from 1798 until 1808.

Monticello   Aug. 12.07.

Dear brother

I did not recieve your letter of July 9 till the 8th. inst. and now, by the first post inclose you 20.D. to pay for the clover and greenswerd seed; which goes by post to Warren. The greenswerd seed I wish to have here; but the white clover seed is to go to Bedford. I must therefore get you to make interest with Mr. Crouch to have it conveyed to the care of Mr. Brown mercht. of Lynchburg for Burgess Griffin at Poplar Forest.[1] This he can do I expect by his batteaux which go to Lynchburg.

Our sister Marks[2] arrived here last night and we shall be happy to see you also. I salute you affectionately.

Th:Jefferson

[1]Burgess Griffin was an overseer at Poplar Forest, Jefferson's farm in Bedford County.

[2]Anna Scott (Mrs. Hastings) Marks was Randolph's twin sister. The Markses lived in Louisa County, adjacent to Albemarle County on the east.

Dr brother

I would Esteem it as a singular favour of you if you Would be so Good as to lend us your Gigg harness to go as fare as charlotte as one of My wifes brothers lays like to dye and she has a great desire to go and see him and they shall be reterned safe back a gane as soon as she gits back Which Will be in seven or Eight days. My Wife Joins me in love to you and family.—

I am Dr brother
yr Most affectionately
Rh:Jefferson
Decemr 7, '09

[Addressed.] Mr. Thomas Jefferson
Pr Squire[1]

---

[1]Squire had been inherited "as a boy" by Randolph Jefferson from the estate of his father.

Thomas Jefferson to Randolph Jefferson

Monticello   Dec. 8. 09.

Dear brother

I send by Squire the Gigg harness, and shall be very happy if after your return, instead of sending it you would avail yourself of it to pay us a visit here with my sister. She promised me a visit in the spring but the distance is too short to require it to be put off to so remote a period. Perhaps you might find an absence from home during winter less inconvenient than after the operations of the farm and garden shall have been begun in the Spring. However we shall be happy to see you both at your own best convenience. In the mean time accept for both the assurances of my affectionate esteem.

Th:Jefferson

Randolph Jefferson to Thomas Jefferson

Stoney point   June 8 1810

Dear brother

I have this Moment Met with your Waggoner Who tells Me that you are Well. I have expected for some time to of received a letter from you—but have not received one yet. I expected you Were Gone to Richmond, before this agreable to What you told Me Which I expected Was the reason of My Not Gitting one from you, I should of bin over before this but have bin very much put to it to git Iron to make an axiltree to my Gigg and have not got any yet I understand there is some landed at Capt. pattersons Grocery at Warren With in a few days past, and I intend Going up there tomorrow Morning to try and Git some for that perpose, and if I should git any, it Wont be Very long before We Will be over but at this time, it is out of My power to fix on any Certain time. You Will excuse My scribble.—

I am dear brother yr Most affectionately
Rh;Jefferson

[Addressed] Mr. Thomas Jefferson
            By Jerry[1]   Monticello

---

[1]Jerry was a trusted Monticello slave who had been inherited from Peter Jefferson's estate.

Thomas Jefferson to Randolph Jefferson

Monticello   June 11.10.

Dear brother

Yours of the 8th. is recieved. I thought it had been agreed between us that I should give you information only when I should be notified of the time of my attendance in Richmond, and that not writing would be evidence to you of my continuance at home. In fact my journey to Richmond is put off to the Fall. I shall therefore be at home till the middle of July, about which time I shall go to Bedford,[1] and shall hope to see you and my sister[2] here before I set out. My absence on that journey will be of about a month. All here are well and join in wishes and salutations to you both.

Affectionately yours
Th:Jefferson

[1]Thomas Jefferson did not depart for Poplar Forest until August 22; there is no evidence in his Memorandum Books that he visited Randolph at Snowden on this trip. Jefferson went to Richmond in the fall, and in December he made a second trip to Poplar Forest.

[2]This is Mitchie B. Pryor, Randolph's second wife. They were married sometime after the death of his first wife, probably in 1809.

Monticello   Sep. 6. 11.

Dear brother

Our worthy sister Carr has at length yielded to the wasting complaint which has for two or three years been gaining upon her.[1] Without any increase of pain, or any other than her gradual decay, she expired three days ago, and was yesterday deposited here by the side of the companion who had been taken from her 38. years before. She had the happiness, and it is a great one, of seeing all her children become worthy and respectable members of society and enjoying the esteem of all. Present my best respects to my sister and be assured of my constant affection.

Th:Jefferson

[1]Martha Jefferson (Mrs. Dabney) Carr died at Monticello on September 3. She was buried beside her husband in the Monticello graveyard on September 5.

Randolph Jefferson to Thomas Jefferson

Octr. 6:11

Dear brother.— —

    I Received yours of the twenty six of last month and am extremly sorry to hear of My sisters death and Would of bin over but it was not raly in My power but it is What we may all expect to come to either later or sooner. I Got Mr. Pryor to call and leave this letter for me as he Was Going to albemarle court and recommended it to him to Make Montocello his first days stage.[1] I intend coming over some time next Month Which I expect will be towards the last of the month as I shall be very busy in gitting My crop of Wheat down to Richmond and sowing My present crop you will not forget to take care of my puppy if you have not given him a Way to any one I expect by this time he Must be large.[2] I have Just Got over a very severe tack of the Gravil I could Not of survived Many ours had I not Got releaf from a physician immidately.[3] My Wife and family presents there respects to you and family. I am yrs

affectionately
Rh;Jefferson

[1]This was probably Zachariah Pryor, a brother of Randolph's second wife, Mitchie B. Pryor Jefferson.

[2]This dog had been sent to Monticello to be bred to one of Jefferson's shepherd dogs.

[3]Randolph appears to have suffered from an attack of kidney stones.

Monticello   Jan. 14. 12.

Dear brother

When I saw you last I mentioned to you that among a stock of family medicines and conveniences which I laid in by the advice of Dr. Wistar[1] when I left Philadelphia he had put up, I thought, some bougies[2] of better form than common. On searching I have found one of them, which I now send you. Doctr. Walker will be the best judge of it's merit. Should you have a return of your complaint I hope you will by all means follow his judicious advice of using the lunar caustic, as the only means of giving permanent relief, and of ensuring a continuance of life. In his hands the operation will be a safe, and altho' the pain will be great, yet we should make up our minds to the sufferings we are doomed to meet, and meet them with firmness and patience.

On my arrival here I found a letter announcing the death of Mr. Marks.[3] I sent for our sister as soon as she could leave that neighborhood, and she is now here; but in very low health indeed, and scarcely able to walk about the house.

I had the opportunity yesterday of sending your watch to Richmond. Present my respects to my sister.

Yours affectionately
Th:Jefferson

[1]Dr. Caspar Wistar was a friend of Jefferson and an eminent Philadelphia physician.

[2]A bougie was an instrument utilized to give relief from urinary ailments. Generally a flexible cylinder, probably of elastic gum, variable in size, it was introduced through the urethra past the obstruction. Jefferson is not reported as using bougies at this time.

[3]Hastings Marks, Randolph and Thomas's brother-in-law, died at his Louisa County home.

Woodlawn[1]   Feby 8:12

Dear brother.—

I received yours of the 6 instant, and am extreemly oblige to you for the things you Were so kind as to send Me. Which came to hand safe, I have not had a tetch of My complaint sence I saw you, and have greatly mended in flesh. I have rode down to snowden[2] on horse back and I found it not disagree a tall with Me, tho I rode Very slow, and once I went down in the gigg all appeard to a gree exceedingly well with me so far. As soon as the roads gits in good order we Will come over I expect it will be the last of next Month or the first of april, I am Very sorry to hear of My sister Marks low state of health, but hope she Will recover after a little time after the weather Gits a little Warmer,[3] if My health should continue to keep as it is I will endeavour to come over next Month. If your shepards bitch[4] has any More puppys I must Git the favour of you to save Me one dog puppy. My Wife and family Joins in love and Respect to all of you.

I am your Most affectionatly.—
Rh;Jefferson

N B If you sent my watch to Fast Bender it is More then probable that she went to the Flames with the rest of the Watches in his shop as his shop Were burnt about the eighttenth of Jany.— — —

[1]Woodlawn was probably the Buckingham County home of Randolph's second wife.

[2]Snowden was Randolph Jefferson's farm in Buckingham County across the James River from Scott's Ferry.

[3]Anna Scott Marks recovered and lived until July 6, 1828.

[4]This dog was probably one of the pair of "shepherd dogs" sent Jefferson by Lafayette in 1809 and not a descendant of the Briard breed purchased in France.

Dear brother

I have bin informd by Mr. R: patteson who has Just got up from Richmond a day or two past that MY Watch is safe and in the possession of Mr. Fass Bender will you be so good as to send down for her by some person who will be going down shortly that can be depended on to bring her up safe as I expect we shall be over early in May Which time the roads Will be in good order to travil and as soon as they are I shall set of over I have one request to ask of you and that is if your bitch has any more puppys by her at this time I would thank you to save Me a dog if you have Not ingaged them to any other person sence you Went from heare I have recovered my health in a great Measure to What I was but at times feel the simtoms but after a day or two it leavs Me I have not put a drop of any kind of spirits in My Mouth sence I saw you[1] Neither have I seen Doctor Walker sence I received your letter. My Wife Joins Me in love and Respect to you and family. I am Dear brother

your most affectionatily.—
Rh:Jefferson
april 13: 1812

[Addressed] Mr: Thomas:Jefferson
Politeness Mr: R:Bell
Monticello

---

[1]Randolph's statement about his consumption of "spirits" is of interest for it is the only such reference indicating that he may have had a drinking problem.

Randolph Jefferson to Thomas Jefferson

Dear Brother

    I have sent Squire over to you for the garden seeds you were so kind as to promise us. What ever you can best spare we are now living at home and would be happy to see you and familey When ever convenient we are at this time at woodlawn on account of Mrs. pryors illness but she is much Mendid on account of that we shall leave this in a day or two.[1] My Wife Joins me in love to you and family. I am Dear brother

yr Most affectionately.—
Rh; Jefferson
Feby 24: 1813

P S You will be please to
write to me by Squire

[Addressed] Thomas Jefferson eqr.
           pr Squire
           Monticello

---

[1]This was no doubt Randolph's mother-in-law, Mrs. David Pryor.

Mar. 2.13.

Dear brother

Having been from home the last fall during most of the season for saving seeds, I find on examination that my gardener has made a very scanty provision. Of that however I send enough to put you in stock: to wit Early Frame peas, Ledman's peas, long haricots, red haricots, grey snaps Lima beans, carrots, parsneps, salsafia, spinach, Sprout kale, tomatas.[1] I have sent you none of the following because all your neighbors can furnish them, and my own stock is short. To wit Lettuce radish, cucumbers, squashes, cabbages, turneps. Mrs. Randolph[2] makes up some flower seeds for my sister. I do not expect to go to Bedford till late in April. If by that time I learn that the road from Mr. Hudson's to Scott's ferry[3] is passable I will certainly call on you. I meant to have done it as I returned in November last, but learned that the boat at that ferry was gone, and that I would not be able to cross there. All here are well and salute my sister and yourself, disappointed that you did not come for the seeds. Adieu

Yours affectionately
Th:Jefferson

[1]For the variety of vegetables grown in the Monticello garden, see *Thomas Jefferson's Garden Book*, annotated by Edwin M. Betts (Philadelphia, 1944).

[2]Martha Jefferson (Mrs. Thomas Mann) Randolph.

[3]Scott's Ferry was located on the James River in the vicinity of present Scottsville.

Thomas Jefferson to Randolph Jefferson

Monticello   May 25.13

Dear brother

   Supposing the shad season not to be quite over, and
that in hauling for them they catch some carp, I send
the bearer with a cart and cask to procure for me as
many living carp as he can to stock my fishpond.[1] I
should not regard his staying a day or two extra, if it
would give a reasonable hope of furnishing a supply. He
is furnished with money to pay for the carp, for which I
have always given the same price as for shad, should he
not be able to lay out the whole in carp he may bring us
3. or 4. shad if he can get them. I shall be able to give
you the spinning Jenny which I carried to Bedford.[2] It
is a very fine one of 12. spindles. I am obliged to make a
larger one for that place, and the cart which carries it up
shall bring the one there to Snowden on it's return. You
will have to send a person here to learn to use it, which
may take them a fortnight. But that need not be till I
return from Bedford, for which place I shall set out the
day after our court, this day fortnight, or very soon after.
I will go by Snowden if I can; but certainly will return
that way, on condition you will previously re-open the
old road to the old smith's shop. You will never find a
more leisure time for your people to do that than the
present. In conversing with your son Lilburne, I found
that he would prefer employing himself in reading and
improving his mind rather than in being idle.[3] It is late
for him to begin, but he has still time enough, to acquire such a degree of information as may make him a
very useful and respectable member of society. I formed

a favorable opinion of his understanding. If both you
and he approve of it, I think he had better come and
pass some time here. I can put him on a course of useful
reading adapted to his age. This would be of geography,
history, agriculture, and natural philosophy: as soon as
you and he can make up your minds, he had better
come without delay, as he has not a day to lose. He can
pursue his reading as well while I am absent in Bedford, as when here.

Reflecting on the manner of managing your very
valuable farm, I thought I would suggest the following
which appears to me the best, and of which you will
consider.[4] To form your lowgrounds into two divisions,
one of them to be in wheat, and the other to be half corn
and half red clover, shifting them every year. Then to
form your highlands into three divisions, one to be in
wheat and the other two in red clover, shifting them
from year to year. In this way your low ground fields
would be in corn but once in 4. years, in wheat every
other year, and in clover every fourth year: and your
highland in wheat once in every three years, and in clover two years in every three. They would improve wonderfully fast in this way, and increase your produce of
wheat and corn every year. If it should be found that the
low grounds should in this way become too rich for
wheat, instead of putting them every fourth year into
clover, you might put them that year into oats. Your annual crop would then be half your low grounds in
wheat, a fourth in corn, and a fourth in oats or clover:
and one third of your highland in wheat, and two thirds
in clover; and so on for ever, and for ever improving. I

suggest this for your consideration. Present me affectionately to my sister, and be assured yourself of my constant and brotherly attachment.

Th:Jefferson

[1]Thomas Jefferson maintained several fishponds at Monticello for storing fish. The only one whose location is known is on the west lawn.

[2]For Jefferson's interest in spinning and weaving, see *Thomas Jefferson's Farm Book*, ed. Edwin M. Betts (Philadelphia, 1953; reprinted Charlottesville, Va., 1977), pp. 464–95.

[3]James Lilburne Jefferson was the fifth child and youngest son of Randolph Jefferson and his first wife, Anne Jefferson Lewis Jefferson. He was the only one of Randolph's children in whose education Thomas Jefferson appears to have taken an active interest.

[4]Jefferson frequently gave advice to members of his family on a myriad of subjects including marriage, childbearing, gambling, fox hunting, etc.

Dear brother

Monticello May 25.13

Supposing the shad season not to be quite over, and that in hauling for them they catch some carp, I send the bearer with a cart and cask to procure for me as many living carp as he can to stock my fishpond. I should not regard his staying a day or two extra, if it would give a reasonable hope of furnishing a supply. he is furnished with money to pay for the carp, for which I have always given the same price as for shad. should he not be able to lay out the whole in carp he may bring us 3. or 4. shad if he can get them.   I shall be able to give you the spinning Jenny which I carried to Bedford. it is a very fine one of 12. spindles. I am obliged to make a larger one for that place, and the cart which carries it up shall bring the one there to Snowden on it's return. you will have to send a person here to learn to use it, which may take them a fortnight. but that need not be till I return from Bedford, for which place I shall set out the day after our court, this day fortnight, or very soon after. I will go by Snowden if I can; but certainly will return that way, on condition you will previously re-open the old road to the old smith's shop. you will never find a more leisure time for your people to do that than the present. in conversing with your son Lilburne, I found that he would prefer employing himself in reading and improving his mind rather than in being idle. it is late for him to begin, but he has still time enough, to acquire such a degree of information as may make him a very useful & respectable member of society. I formed a favorable opinion of his understanding. if both you & he approve of it. I think he had better come and pass some time here. I can put him on a course of useful reading adapted to his age

Randolph Jefferson

Thomas Jefferson to Randolph Jefferson, May 25, 1813. (Courtesy of the Tracy W. McGregor Library, University of Virginia)

this would be of geography, history, agriculture, & natural philosophy. as soon as you and he can make up your minds, he had better come without delay, as he has not a day to lose. he can pursue his reading as well while I am absent in Bedford, as when here.

Reflecting on the manner of managing your very valuable farm, I thought I would suggest the following which appears to me the best, & of which you will consider. to form your lowgrounds into two divisions, one of them to be in wheat, and the other to be half corn & half red clover, shifting them every year. then to form your highlands into three divisions; one to be in wheat, & the other two in red clover, shifting them from year to year. in this way your lowground fields would be in corn but once in 4. years, in wheat every other year, and in clover every fourth year: and your highland in wheat once in every three years, and in clover two years in every three. they would improve wonderfully fast in this way, and increase your produce of wheat & corn every year. if it should be found that the lowgrounds should in this way become too rich for wheat, instead of putting them every fourth year into clover, you might put them that year into oats. your annual crops would then be half your lowgrounds in wheat, a fourth in corn, and a fourth in oats or clover: and one third of your highland in wheat, and two thirds in clover, and so on for ever, and for ever improving. I suggest this for your consideration. present me affectionately to my sister, and be assured yourself of my constant & brotherly attachment.

Th Jefferson

Dear Brother   May 26th 1813.

I recieved your friendly letter
by the boy they catch no shad a tall
at this time so that I have sent James
up to Warren to try and procure some
carp for you and have wrote to mr B
rown about them if it is in his power
to git any to furnish your boy with what
you directed him to bring in the barrel a
live I have understood they catch a num
ber there every night in the mill race I
will endeavour to fix Lilburne as soon
as possible and send him agreable to your
request and hope he will endeavour to
improve himself by applying
closely to his book I will do my bes
t to have the rode put in better order
a gainst you come along as fare as the
shop on the rode we are extreemly oblige to
you in respect to the spining ginney as

Randolph Jefferson to Thomas Jefferson, May 26, 1813.
(Courtesy of the Tracy W. McGregor Library, University of
Virginia)

letting your boy come by and leaveing
it with us as it was more then we could
of ask'd of you at any rate or expected
I am extreemly obliged to you for your advi
ce as to manageing my farm but am a
fraid it will be two great an undertak
ing for me your method I highly appro
ve of I hope Mr Brown will furnish you
with the carp if they catch any you will
be so good as to tell my sister Marks that
we shall be extreemly happy to see her h
ear and that I will return with her if
she will come over my wife joins with
me in love to you and family.—
p S dont be in dred of   I am with the
the old rode I will have   warmest Esteem
that put in good order
a gainst you come a long and regard your
for you.—   sincearly.—

                                        Th; Jefferson

41

Randolph Jefferson to Thomas Jefferson

May the 26:1813

Dear Brother

I received your friendly letter by the boy they catch
no shad a tall at this time so that I have sent James[1] up
to Warren to try and procure some carp for you and
have wrote to Mr. Brown a bout them if it is in his
power to git any to fernish your boy With What you de-
rected him to bring in the barril a live I have understood they cetch a Number there every Night in the
Mill race. I will endeavour to fix Lilburne as soon as
possible and send him a greable to your request and
hope he Will endeavour to improve him self by applying
closely to his book. I will do My best to have the rode
put in better order a gainst you come a long as fare as
the shop on the rode. We are extreemly oblige to you in
respect to the spining ginney as letting your boy come
by and leaveing it with us as it Was more then We could
of asked of you at any rate or expected. I am extreemly
oblige to you for your advice as to Managing My farm
but am a fraid it Will be two great an undertakeng for
Me. Your Method I highly approve of I hope Mr.
Brown Will fernish you with the carp if they cetch any.
You Will be so good as to tell My sister Marks that We
shall be extreemly happy to see her hear and that I will
retern With her if she Will come over. My Wife Joins
With me in love to you and family.—

I am With the Warmest Esteem and
regard your cincearly.—

Rh;Jefferson

May 26, 1813

p s dont be in dred of the old
rode I will have that put in
good order a gainst you come a
long for you.— —

[1]James was one of Randolph's slaves.

Monticello   June 20.13.

Dear brother

The unexpected difficulties of bringing water to my saw mill and threshing machine, and the necessity of doing it before harvest, have obliged me to put off my visit to Bedford till after harvest. The spinning Jenny for Bedford is now ready but will not be sent until I go. While it is here it offers a good opportunity for your spinner to learn upon it. After it is gone there will be no idle machine for a learner to practice on. I send the bearer therefore to inform you of this, that you may not lose the opportunity of getting the person taught whom you intend to employ in that way. I should think she had better come immediately, as it will require a month or more to become perfect in roving[1] and spinning. By the time she is taught, the machine will be off to Bedford, and the cart which carries it will return by Snowden and leave the 12. spindle machine there, on which she may go to work immediately. This will be early in August. I do not know whether I can call on you as I go. I will if I can, but certainly will as I return. Is your road cleared out?

My sister desired that when I should send her seeds of any kind I would give her directions how to plant and cultivate them. Knowing that there was an excellent gardening book published at Washington, I wrote for one for her, which I now inclose.[2] She will there see what is to be done with every kind of plant every month in the year. I have written an index at the end that she may find any particular article more readily: and not to embarras her with such an immense number of articles

which are not wanting in common gardens, I have
added a paper with a list of those I tend in my garden,
and the times when I plant them. The season being
over for planting everything but the Gerkin, I send her
a few seeds of them. She will not find the term Gerkin
in the book. It is that by which we distinguish the very
small pickling cucumber. Affectionate salutations to you
both.

Th:Jefferson

[1]To rove is to draw out and twist slightly, as slivers of wool or cotton.
before spinning.

[2]John Gardiner and David Hepburn, *The American Gardener, Containing Ample Directions for Working a Kitchen Garden. . .* (Washington, D.C., 1804).

Snowden   June 21:1813

Dear Brother

I Received your letter by James and also the book Which you sent: My wife is extreemly oblige to you for your present and is Very much pleased With it. The girl We Will send on the course of a Week[1] We have Not a Woman except a girl of twelve or fourteen years old but What has children. We expected the reason of your not coming on Was on account of the weathers being so worm but shall look for you certainly on your retern from bedford. My Wife is Very Much indesposed at present. We shall certainly expect My sister Marks over this summer. Lilburne has goind the Volunteers but expect he Will be over by the midle of July. I wrote very pressingly to Capt. Brown by your boy in respect to the carp for you but found it was all in Vane from What James tells Me he got none if you should Not conclude to come this Way going up I would be extreemly oblige to you to Mark out the ram to your overseer and I will send up this fall for him as soon as the Weather gits cool so that he can be brought With safety. My Wife goins Me in love and respect to all the family.

I am Dr brother
your Most affectionately.—
Rh:Jefferson

[1]Randolph sent Fanny, one of his slaves.

Randolph Jefferson to Thomas Jefferson

Dear brother

I have sent the girl by Squire and hope she Will answer to learn and should of sent her before but we have
bin so very busy about my Wheat that I could Not spare
a hand out of the field to bring her and Would be Very
Much oblige to you to put her under one of the grone
hands to keep her in good order. I suppose We May
send for her in three or four Weeks I would be glad you
Would let us know Whether you can come by. We are
all Well heare My Wife Joins Me in love to the family

I am Dr brother
your Most affectionately . . . —
Rh Jefferson

Monticello   July 12.13.

Dear brother

Your's is recieved by Squire, and the girl begins this
morning the first necessary branch, which is roving, or
spinning into candlewick to prepare it for the spinning
Jenny. This will take her some days, more or less, according to her aptness, and then she will commence on
the Jenny. As she appears rather young, it will probably
take her a month or 6. weeks to learn well enough to be
relied on for carrying it on herself where she can have
no further instruction. However I will by any opportunity which occurs let you know her progress and when
you may send for her. It will be near a month before I
shall be able to set out for Bedford, and uncertain
whether I can go by Snowden or not; but if I do not, I
will certainly return by there, and the machine will go
to you at the same time;[1] about which time I imagine it
will be best that your girle should meet it there, con-
tinuing to spin here till then, that she may be more perfect. With affectionate salutations to my sister and yourself accept my adieux.

Th:Jefferson

[1]Jefferson stopped at Snowden on September 14 while en route from
Poplar Forest to Monticello.

Randolph Jefferson to Thomas Jefferson

august 8th:1813

Dear brother

I have sent Squire over to see Whether I could borrow forty dollers of you as I am compelled to have as Much at Court if it is possible to borrow as Much of you Which shall certainly be replaced a gane in three weaks Which Will be a bout the time I shall dispose of My crop of Wheat and will take extreemly kind of you if it is in your power to help Me at this time Which I shall feel My self under Many obligations to you for the loan of.[1] Be pleased to discharge Squire as soon as possible and Would be glad to heare how Fanny comes on. My Wife goins Me in love to you and the family.—

I am your affectionately
yours.—
Rh Jefferson

[1]The August 8 entry in Jefferson's Memorandum Books reads: "Inclosed to my brother 40.D. of which he asks a loan."

Thomas Jefferson to Randolph Jefferson

Monticello   Aug.8.13.

Dear brother

Your letter of yesterday found me unprovided with the sum you desired; but I have been able to borrow it among our merchants who are not much better off than others, all business being at a stand. We are experiencing the most calamitous year known since 1755. The ground has been wet but once since the 14th. of April. My wheat yielded but a third of an ordinary crop, about treble the seed. Of 230. acres of corn, about 15. acres may make 2. or 3. barrels to the acre; and about 215. acres will not produce a single ear; not half of it will tassil, a great deal not 2. feet high. We usually make about 7. or 800. barrels; we shall certainly not make above 30. I shall be obliged to drive all my stock to Bedford to be wintered, and to buy 400. barrels of corn for bread for my people.

Your girl comes on tolerably well. She was some time learning to rove, for without good roving there cannot be good spinning. She has been sometime spinning, and by the time of my return from Bedford, when the machine will be carried to you, she will be able to spin by herself. The time of my going is yet unfixed. It may be within a week, or not within 2. or 3. weeks. My route is equally uncertain; but if I do not go by Snowden I will certainly return by it. Present my respects to my sister. Ever affectionately yours

Th:Jefferson

P. S. Do not think of selling your wheat till the winter drives off the blockading ships when it will bring a good price.

Thomas Jefferson to Randolph Jefferson

Poplar Forest   Sep. 8.13.

Dear brother

The cart sets out this morning with your spinning
Jenny in perfect order, and will deliver it I hope safe
from accident. According to present appearances I may
leave this on Saturday morning, and if in time to get to
Noah Flood's I may be with you to dinner on Sunday,[1]
but if I get only to Henry Flood's I shall dine at
Gibson's and be with you on Sunday evening; and it is
yet possible I may be detained here till Sunday. My best
affections to my sister and yourself.

Th:Jefferson

[1]Noah Flood's Buckingham County ordinary was situated approxi-
mately thirty-two miles southwest of Warren on the road from Poplar
Forest to Monticello.

Dear Brother

I would be greatly oblige to you if Mr. Randolph has reternd home from Richmond if you Will be so good as to ask him to send old Stephen[1] over With My Watch as I am at the greatest loss in the World for the Want of her and at the same time Would take it a great favour of you to send the bitch by him that you Were so good as to give Me When I was over as I have a great desire to see her. I have Waited With all the patience I am Master of expecting Stephen over for three weaks and he has Not come yet and I suppose it is on account of Mr. Randolphs Not reterning home from Richmond yet if Mr. Randolph has not reternd Stephen May Wait and as soon as he gits back you Will be pleased to send Stephen over With My Watch and bitch as it is out of My power to leave home at this time. We are all Well heare at present. My Wife Joins Me in love to you and family

I am your Most affectionately
Rh:Jefferson
Decemr 29:14

[1]Stephen was a hired hand of Thomas Mann Randolph.

Snowden   February 13:1815

Dear brother.—

I have concluded to send over Squire, after the bitch that you was so good to give me, when I was over as I should be extreemly hapy to git her, if she has not pupt, or if she has and he can Make out to bring her and some of the pupies. I can send over for the rest at Esther, without Mr. Randolph will let old Stephen come over and bring the rest for Me. If the bitch has no more then too Squire can bring them him self, I have Waited expecting to see stephen every day, but the reason I suppose his not coming is that Mr. Randolph has not reternd yet from below. As for My Watch I have bin without her so long that I am intirely Weand from her, however if Mr. Randolph should of reternd and brought her, I should be extreemly happy once More to receive her agane. I would be extreemly oblige to you for a few science, of your good fruit, of apple and cherry. If it should not be too late to moove them Now, or any other fruit that you Would oblige Me With, that you have to spare also a few cabbage seed and ice lettuce seed. If it is but one half spoon full provided you have as Many to spare Without disfernishing yourself. I expect I shall be summonsed over to March court on account of Randolph[1] and Craven patons[2] sute in albemarle court. I am at the greatest loss immagenable for the Want of My Watch. If Mr. Randolph has not reternd yet I shall be oblige to send down to Verina but I am still in hopes there Will Not be any occasion to do that, as he Must certainly have reternd long before this time.[3] My Wife

February 13, 1815

Joins Me in love and respect to you and family. I am your most affectionately. — — —

Rh;Jefferson

Do pray Sir give Squire such derections inrespect to the bitch as you think Most Necessary and you Will Very Much oblige

your Most affectionately. Rh:Jefferson

[Note in Thomas Jefferson's hand] Apples, cherries, cabbage, ice lettuce.

¹This was probably Thomas Mann Randolph.

²Craven Peyton was a merchant in Milton, the small village that lay several miles southeast of Monticello. He married Jane Jefferson Lewis, a daughter of Randolph's sister Lucy Jefferson (Mrs. Charles Lilburne) Lewis.

³Varina was a plantation in Goochland County owned by Thomas Mann Randolph.

Thomas Jefferson to Randolph Jefferson

Monticello   Feb. 16.15

Dear brother

After several disappointments in getting your watch from Richmond, I recieved her a week ago. I sent for Stephen, who came to me and pretended to be sick. Finding he did not mean to go to Snowden I had concluded to send her to you in a day or two, when Squire arrived. She appears to have gone well since I have had her, except a little too fast. With respect to Stephen Mr. Randolph got rid of him long ago. I am told he stays now at North Milton or somewhere there. He talks of going down the country to live. I send you some green curled Savoy cabbage seed. I have no ice lettuce, but send you what I think better the white loaf lettuce. The ice lettuce does not do well in a dry season. I send you also some sprout kale, the finest winter vegetable we have. Sow it and plant it as cabbage, but let it stand out all winter. It will give sprouts from the first of December to April. The bitch I had given you was caught in the very act of eating a sheep which she had killed. She was immediately hung, and as we had a fine litter at the same time from another bitch, I preserved one of them for you, which Squire is now gone for and will carry over to you.—I have for some years so entirely neglected my fruit trees that I have nothing in my nursery but refuse stuff, unknown and of no value. There is a rumor here of peace; but that we shall have peace in the spring I have little doubt. I hold up my flour therefore till May. Present my compliments to my sister and be assured of my sincere affections.

Th:Jefferson

Feb. 17. The news of peace is confirmed since yesterday so that I have little doubt of it. Wheat and tobo. will be immediately at a good price. Corn which was at 27/ at Richmond will tumble down instantly, because their supplies which are always from the great corn country of Rappahanoc will come round by water now freely and immediately.

Randolph Jefferson to Thomas Jefferson

April 2:15

Dear brother

My sister Marks arrived heare very safe on friday evening, but Was verry Much fatigued after her Jorney. I
have got pritty Well a gane, but Extreemly Week at this
time, Scarce able to Walk. I am exceedingly oblige to
you for the things you sent Me. I have just sold to
charles S: Scott, 70 acres of My low grounds at a
hundred dollers pr acre, for Which he is to Make the
first payment a bout the twelfth of this Month, Which
Will take Me out of debt With every Man that I am in-
volved With and Which Will enable me to keep all My
Slaves as long as I live. The Next payment he is to
Make me this time twelve Months. I will try and take a
ride over some time this summer if my health will permit. The river is so high that they cant put in the sane
to fish, but as soon as the river gits down so as they
ketch any We will immidiately send you over a parcel
by Squire. My Wife Joins Me in love and affection to
you and family.— —I am you Most affectionately

Rh;Jefferson

p s Jefferson and young Wilson Nicholas took a ride to
see me on saterday but made no stay of account With us
for the first time.—[1]

[1]Thomas Jefferson Randolph was Randolph's nephew, the son of
Martha Jefferson and Thomas Mann Randolph. Wilson Cary Nicholas was the son of Wilson Cary Nicholas, Sr., of Warren. Thomas
Jefferson Randolph married Nicholas's sister Jane Hollins Nicholas
in 1815.

Thomas Jefferson to Randolph Jefferson

Monticello   June 23.15.

Dear brother

I lent you some years ago the harness of our family gigg, until you could get one made for your own.[1] Mrs. Marks tells me your gigg is now demolished and out of use. Mine has been used with one of our chariot harness. A neighbor asks the loan of it to go on a journey, and if we let one of our set of harness go, we shall not be able to use the carriage until his return which will be very distant. Under these circumstances I send the bearer to ask the return of the harness I lent you, in order to accomodate my neighbor. Present my respects to my sister and be assured of my best affections.

Th:Jefferson

[1]See Randolph Jefferson to Thomas Jefferson, December 7, 1809.

Dear brother

I Received yours by the boy the harness in Which
you were kind enough to lend us Was intirely Worn out
so that they did not scarce las us over to prince
Edward[1] and back. Mr. patteson borrowed our gigg to
go over to the springs and had the harness With the
gigg and they lasted him as far as stanton on his Way to
the springs and there he left them and baught a New
set in Which he gave to us and as our gigg is demolished the harness is of No service to us Now and have
sent them over by your boy Which you are Very Wel-
com too. Your boy informs us of pore Mrs. Carrs death
Which I am extreemly sorry to heare of. We are Very
busy at this time in our harvest Which I expect Will be
several days before We shall be able to finish. My Wife
Joins Me in love and respect to you and family.—I remain your Most affectionately.—

Rh:Jefferson
June 23.15

[1]Prince Edward County.